D1716672

LOS ANGELES RAMS

KENNY ABDO

Fly!
An Imprint of Abdo Zoom
abdobooks.com

abdobooks.com

Published by Abdo Zoom, a division of ABDO, P.O. Box 398166, Minneapolis, Minnesota 55439. Copyright © 2022 by Abdo Consulting Group, Inc. International copyrights reserved in all countries. No part of this book may be reproduced in any form without written permission from the publisher. Fly!™ is a trademark and logo of Abdo Zoom.

Printed in the United States of America, North Mankato, Minnesota.
052021
092021

THIS BOOK CONTAINS RECYCLED MATERIALS

Photo Credits: AP Images, Getty Images, Icon Sportswire, iStock, Shutterstock PREMIER
Production Contributors: Kenny Abdo, Jennie Forsberg, Grace Hansen
Design Contributors: Candice Keimig, Neil Klinepier

Library of Congress Control Number: 2020919711

Publisher's Cataloging-in-Publication Data

Names: Abdo, Kenny, author.
Title: Los Angeles Rams / by Kenny Abdo
Description: Minneapolis, Minnesota : Abdo Zoom, 2022 | Series: NFL teams |
    Includes online resources and index.
Identifiers: ISBN 9781098224691 (lib. bdg.) | ISBN 9781098225636 (ebook) |
    ISBN 9781098226107 (Read-to-Me ebook)
Subjects: LCSH: Los Angeles Rams (Football team : 2016-)--Juvenile literature. |
    National Football League--Juvenile literature. | Football teams--Juvenile literature. |
    American football--Juvenile literature. | Professional sports--Juvenile literature.
Classification: DDC 796.33264--dc23

TABLE OF CONTENTS

LOS ANGELES RAMS

Starting back in the 1930s, the Rams have shown power and strength, while butting heads with teams for victories.

From the icy plains of Ohio, to the Gateway Arch of St. Louis, all the way to the sunny west coast, the Rams are the only **franchise** in NFL history to win **championships** for three cities!

KICK OFF

The Rams joined the NFL in 1937. The team was based in Cleveland, Ohio. The Rams played the Detroit Lions in their first game, losing 28-0.

The Rams won their first NFL **championship** in 1945. They beat Washington in below freezing temperatures!

The Rams headed to warmer weather in 1946. Owner Dan Reeves moved the team to Los Angeles. The Rams won the 1951 NFL **championship** against the Browns 24-17.

13

TEAM RECAPS

The Rams played in **Super Bowl** XIV, but lost a tough game to the Steelers 31–19. With no Big Game visits within the next 15 years, the team moved to Saint Louis, Missouri.

The Rams again appeared at **Super Bowl** XXXIV. They beat the Tennessee Titans 23–16! The Rams made it back to the Super Bowl two years later, but lost to the New England Patriots 20–17.

Los Angeles got its team back when the Rams relocated again in 2016. The Rams ended the season with a 4-12 record, after letting head coach Jeff Fisher go midseason.

The Rams closed out the 2018 season with a 13-3 record and a trip to the **Super Bowl**! Unfortunately, they lost to the New England Patriots 13-3.

The Rams landed a 10-6 record for the 2020 season. They beat the Seahawks 30-20 in the **Wild Card** playoff game, but lost to the Packers in the **divisional** playoffs.

23

HALL OF FAME

Bob Waterfield wore many hats with the Rams. He was a place kicker, punter, and defensive end. As **quarterback**, Waterfield racked up 11,849 passing yards, 97 passing touchdowns, and 573 points in his eight seasons with the Rams.

Waterfield became the first Rams player to join the Pro Football Hall of Fame in 1965.

During his seven years with the Rams, Marshall Faulk was named NFL Offensive Player of Year three times and **MVP** once! He helped the Rams become **Super Bowl** champions at XXXIV. Faulk was **inducted** into the Pro Football Hall of Fame in 2011.

Kurt Warner was the Rams' **quarterback** for five years. He led the team to victory at **Super Bowl** XXXIV where he set a record by throwing more than 400 yards in the Big Game. He was also the first QB to pass 40 touchdowns and win a Super Bowl in the same season. Warner was **inducted** into the Pro Football Hall of Fame in 2017.

GLOSSARY

championship – a game held to find a first-place winner.

division – a group of teams who compete against each other for a championship.

franchise – a professional sports team.

induct – to admit someone as a member of an organization.

MVP – short for "most valuable player," an award given in sports to a player who has performed the best in a game or series.

quarterback (QB) – the player on the offensive team that directs teammates in their play.

Super Bowl – the NFL championship game, played once a year.

Wild Card Round – the first round of the playoffs. Each of the two conferences send four division champions and three wild-card teams to its postseason.

ONLINE RESOURCES

Booklinks
NONFICTION NETWORK
FREE! ONLINE NONFICTION RESOURCES

To learn more about the Los Angeles Rams, please visit **abdobooklinks.com** or scan this QR code. These links are routinely monitored and updated to provide the most current information available.

INDEX